LOFTS 2

LOFTS 2

Edited by Cristina Paredes Benítez

COLLINS|DESIGN

An Imprint of HarperCollins*Publishers*

First Edition

First edition published in 2006 by:
Loft Publications
Via Laietana 32 4.º of. 104
08003 Barcelona. Spain
Tel.: +34 932 688 088
Fax: +34 932 680 425
www.loftpublications.com

English language edition first published in 2006 by:
Collins Design
An Imprint of HarperCollinsPublishers
10 East 53rd Street
New York, NY 10022
Tel.: (212) 207-7000
Fax: (212) 207-7654
collinsdesign@harpercollins.com
www.harpercollins.com

Distributed throughout the world by:
HarperCollinsPublishers
10 East 53rd Street
New York, NY 10022
Fax: (212) 207-7654

Editor: Paco Asensio
Text: Cristina Paredes Benítez
Art director: Mireia Casanovas Soley
Translation: Heather Bagott
Layout: Diego González

Library of Congress Cataloging-in-Publication Data

Lofts 2: good ideas / edited by Cristina Paredes.—1st ed.
    p. cm.
  ISBN 13: 978-0-06-084729-6 (pbk.)
  ISBN 10: 0-06-084729-8 (pbk.)
  1. Lofts.   2. Interior architecture—History—21st century.
  3. Interior decoration—History—21st century.   I. Title: Lofts two.   II. Paredes, Cristina.
  NA7882.L58 2006
  747'.88314—dc22
                              2005034919

Printed by: Anman Gràfiques del Vallès, Spain.
First Printing, 2006

LOFTS 2

Since the first lofts appeared in Manhattan in the 1950s, the concept has varied and been adapted to the characteristics of contemporary architecture and the needs of present day life. The practice of transforming old factories and warehouses into workshops and living areas has endured until today, and loft living is embraced in towns all over the world. There is greater diversity in the spaces used to create lofts, and even newly built constructions can be found. The evolution of the concept has converted the word "loft" into a synonym for wide open spaces, multifunctional living areas, and state-of-the-art interior design.

The loft's great beauty lies in its unique layout, which can be imaginatively exploited. The majority are characterized by a single open spac,e which facilitates the creation of an individualized interior. The versatility of open spaces also makes renovations less costly than for other types of dwellings. The comparatively great height of these old industrial buildings enables the various interior living areas to be situated on different levels. Panels and partial partitions make creative dividers and permit varying degrees of privacy to suit the occasion or function. Interior design plays an important role in the creation of a genuine loft. The use of colors and the furniture placement can separate areas visually and the preservation of period industrial features such as columns and high ceilings recalls the past life of the structure. Buildings that house newly built lofts accommodate a reasonable distribution of space and services and grant the decorator or owner carte blanche in regard to the interior design.

This book showcases up-to-date projects by prestigious architects and interior designers from all over the world. The attractive and innovative ideas presented are a great source of inspiration as a result of their original design and audacious decoration.

Levels

Loft in São Paulo

Architect: **Brunete Fraccaroli**

☐ The architect Brunete Fraccaroli had no problems in the remodeling of this attractive space, which is bursting with color and freshness. It was agreed that the old structure of columns and iron beams would be maintained, with the simple addition of a mezzanine, where the owner/filmmaker's office and master bedroom could be located. The day area fills the lower floor, housing the kitchen, the main living room, and a small room furnished with a music system and plasma television. The original brick walls have been preserved, which give the interior warmth, and they contrast well with the tempered-glass-sheet panels. These panels are engraved with designs chosen by the owner, which make reference to his profession and can be found throughout the loft, illuminating each of the different zones with colors and reflections. The transparency of this material doesn't interfere with the original architecture and emphasizes the complementary nature of the modifications, as well as showering the loft with light.

Location: São Paulo, Brazil › Completion date: 2003 › Photos: © João Ribeiro

Capitalizing on the impressive height of this loft, the architect has added a mezzanine to gain space. The tempered-glass material introduces visual continuity between the levels.

Old and new intermix easily in an interior
full of industrial reminiscences, resulting
in a warm and hospitable dwelling.

Loft in Bergamo

Architect: Studio Associato Bettinelli

☐ An urban and contemporary ambience emanates from this loft located in the Italian town of Bergamo. The living space is distributed throughout various levels and is characterized by simplicity of décor and high-quality finishes. The living room, which boasts a polished cement floor, is situated between two levels, around an elegant staircase that constitutes the centerpiece of this loft. The décor is reduced to the basics: a sofa and television which are surrounded by books laid out along the floor, creating a strong visual element and serving as a guiderail leading to a plain bedroom with no other divider to set it off. The light that flows into the bedroom is filtered by roller blinds made from lightweight fabric. The topmost level of this loft houses the dining room and kitchen area, which is transformed by athe placement of furniture and freestanding appliances into a flexible and dynamic space. The dining room table is positioned next to the kitchen, where, as in the bedroom, wooden floors contribute to the elegant and hospitable atmosphere.

Location: Bergamo, Italy › Completion date: 2002 › Photos: © Andrea Martiradonna

The dining room table is positioned next to the kitchen. The design
flow of the whole loft creates a functional and elegant space.

The staircase is one of the defining elements of the apartment; its straight lines and clean design create a reference point for the whole interior.

Fraternitat Duplex

Architect: Joan Bach

☐ Simplicity and color are the main themes of this project: a simple, uncluttered apartment with a mezzanine, where the distribution of space is delimited by specially chosen furniture. The predominant colors are red, white, and black, giving the loft and furniture a bold note. The bedroom with en suite bathroom, the kitchen area, and a small balcony are situated on the first level. The apartment enjoys natural light, which flows in through the balcony. The day area comprises the dining room furnished with a modern white table and chairs and a unique standing lamp, the American-style kitchen, and a chesterfield sofa that functions as a living area and lends a classic touch, which contrasts well with the loft's modern aspect. The lightweight metal staircase leading to the mezzanine is a decorative element in itself. This area has a lower ceiling, which gives a cozier feel, and features a lounge with red sofas and a plasma television.

Location: Barcelona, Spain › Completion date: 2003 › Photos: © Jordi Miralles

Two skylights illuminate the upper level, where the mezzanine
is bounded by a single rail, which contributes
to the effect of spatial continuity.

Apartment in Marais

Architect: Guita Maleki & Pascal Cheikh Djavadi

☐ In this loft, located in the Marais quarter of Paris, the great height of the building has been used to advantage in order to accommodate all the functional areas of the apartment. Two of the three levels hold the main elements and the third is a landing between the two floors, where the bathroom and a corridor lined with closets are situated. The loft has a real warmth to it thanks to the preservation of the original wooden beams and the ivory hues. The creative design of the kitchen features a glass wall, which separates it from the living room and serves as a barrier to odor and noise, while contributing a sense of continuity as well as a source of light. The bedroom is on the top floor and therefore makes the most of the sloped roof as a design feature. This level has no walls or panels separating it from the lower level; the only demarcations are the stairwell and handrails, which incorporate shelving to hold books or ornaments.

Location: Paris, France › Completion date: 2002 › Photos: © Solvi do Santos/Omnia

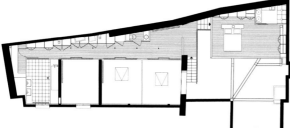

Plans

The lower levels can be observed from the bedroom, which is situated in what was originally the attic. No room is isolated, lending unity to the space.

Van Gelder Loft

Architect: Raphaël Orts, Nicolas Balleriaux

☐ This loft occupies the second and third floors of a typical house in Brussels, providing it with great views over the garden of the adjacent patio. The project goal was to transform an old attic into a luminous and spacious loft, with a sizable lounge, an open kitchen, a desk space, and a large terrace. The functional areas were created by introducing various architectonic volumes, such as the mezzanine, which was built to house the study and the desk. The entrance hall forms another structural space, concealing the kitchen's utility area, while a third area defines the path out to the terrace and frames the exterior views. The wooden floors and the spatial flow resulting from the absence of walls contribute to the homey atmosphere. The mezzanine is an additional light-filled space from which the lower floor can be viewed. The furniture is an imaginative blend of different styles including old and contemporary pieces, combining to create a harmonious and inviting interior.

Location: Brussels, Belgium › Completion date: 2001 › Photos: © Laurent Brandajs

From the mezzanine, the clean and orderly kitchen and dining area can be viewed. The absence of superfluous elements gives the loft vitality.

The bathroom wraps itself around a simple platform, which on one side holds the sink and on the other conceals the shower.

Residence in Surry Hills

Architect: Smart Design Studio

☐ This old building is one of the most emblematic constructions in Surry Hills. It was practically burned to the ground during a fire, and was subsequently used as a workshop for a group of artists. Thus, a total rehabilitation, including important safety measures, was necessary for this project. The place has been converted into an open and flexible space, resulting in a loft with a design that allows it to be used as a commercial space, an office, or a living area. This flexibility enables the owner to live on the higher level and work on the lower one. A feeling of warmth is achieved through the impressive restoration of the stonework, an outstanding feature of the rehabilitation. The bathroom and kitchen are new, modern elements, as is the polished cement tiled floor of the lower level. This modernity contrasts with the stained wooden floor of the upper level and the roof beams. The decoration is modern yet simple and does not detract from the spirit of the original space. One of the oldest buildings in town has thereby regained its original charm.

Location: Surry Hills, New South Wales, Australia › Completion date: 2004 › Photos: © Sharrin Rees

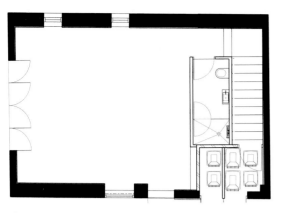

Plans

The kitchen, dining room, living room, and bedroom coexist
in a single space beneath the roof of the two wings.
The absence of tall furniture transmits spatial continuity.

Frankie Loft

Architect: Joan Bach

☐ This small, fresh loft is a fine example of how a functional and attractive apartment can be achieved through good organization of space. The bedroom has been situated on a mezzanine, taking full advantage of the building's high ceilings. The study, which enjoys great natural light, is located below the bedroom and contains a small table and a unique lamp. The living room includes a sofa bed and a small pouf, which serves as a coffee table. The kitchen is situated behind one of the few walls in the loft and is connected to the rest of the space by means of an opening that also serves as a small bar. The wooden floors and the free flow of natural light through the large windows lend the apartment a certain warmth. The color red boosts the vitality of the space and is central to the décor of the apartment, evident in the armchair, curtains, and bedroom. The careful design of the space and the furniture selected make this small loft feel anything but chaotic or cramped.

Location: Barcelona, Spain › Completion date: 2004 › Photos: © Jordi Miralles

The layout of this kitchen suits the small area. The interior space is magnified by the use of white, and the window over the counter establishes visual continuity with the rest of the loft.

RP Apartment

Architect: Daniele Geltrudi

☐ This duplex is located on the top floor of a five-story building lacking in any special architectural value. The loft has been given personality by the architect's decorative scheme—for example, the use of walnut wood, which endows the apartment with a feeling of comfort and warmth. The lower floor boasts a wooden closet with irregular openings that facilitate ventilation, as well as a modern living area with Vitra chairs in representational shapes such as the "coconut." Between the two floors, a unique sculptural element consisting of five gold pillars has pride of place, which, in addition to serving as a focal point, also conveys a fun theatrical effect. The walnut wood staircase leads to a second level, which is characterized by the complex intersection of the different roof planes. This space houses the kitchen, the dining room, and a small balcony, allowing for the flow of natural light. The low-level cupboards and shelving enhance the continuity of the space, while the roof planes add visual interest.

Location: Busto Arsizio, Italy › Completion date: 2003 › Photos: © Andrea Martiradonna

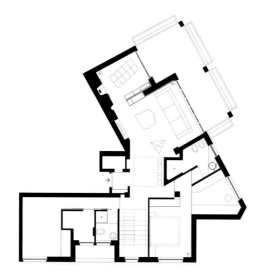
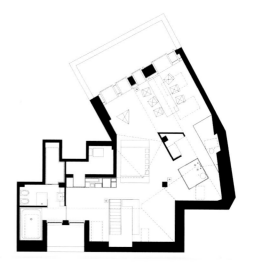

Plans

Duplex in Born

Architect: Joan Pons Forment

☐ This elegant and modern one-bedroom duplex loft is located in the Born quarter of Barcelona, one of the most cosmopolitan and fashionable areas of the city. The hall, kitchen, living room, and dining room come together in a single space on the lower level, with the bathroom and master bedroom upstairs. The black-and-white color scheme is broken up by the presence of grays and the occasional touch of red. The living room is furnished with a comfortable sofa and a white fur rug that provide interesting contrast against the black wall at the other end of the room. A black dining room table sits between the living room and the kitchen, above which hangs a sparkling, chandelier-inspired light fixture. The kitchen, which combines white with steel, fits perfectly with the simplicity of the space, owing to its refined lines. On the upper floor, the studio and bedroom flow into one another and have been designed in harmony with the rest of the loft, employing the same simple lines and somber but elegant furniture.

Location: Barcelona, Spain › Completion date: 2001 › Photos: © Jordi Miralles

The graceful, lightweight staircase takes on a sculptural feel as it contrasts with the white and dark gray color scheme.

The minimalist design of this loft creates an atmosphere that transmits tranquility. The natural light accentuates this effect and can be used imaginatively.

Industrial Details

Loft in Madrid

Architect: Manuel Serrano Arquitectos

☐ The aim of this rehabilitation was to transform an old sculpture workshop into a modern apartment. This amazing transformation has resulted in a spacious loft, which even accommodates an indoor pool in the basement. Some of the original building elements have been preserved, and the exterior has been completely hidden behind white-coated, expanded metal, which also conceals the interior, heightens intimacy, and highlights the patio. The pipes have been left in view, adding to the industrial esthetic evident in the brick walls and metal beams. The height of this former workshop permitted construction of a mezzanine to house the study and bedroom. The use of U-glass translucent panels in the roof, on the mezzanine, and in some areas of the floor facilitates the flow of natural light throughout the apartment from the mezzanine to the basement. The industrial esthetic of the original structure contrasts well with the warm décor that includes parquet flooring and contemporary furniture.

Location: Madrid, Spain › Completion date: 2004 › Photos: © J. Latova

The study benefits from the great quantity of light that flows in through the roof and the floor; glass handrails and use of the color white bring additional lightness to this space.

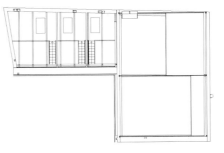

Plans

Noho Loft

Architect: James Slade/Slade Architecture

☐ This attractive New York loft was designed for a young couple, both photographers. In addition to the essential elements of any apartment, the space needed to accommodate a light table and a sizable filing cabinet. The existing space featured high ceilings and columns, which gave the loft personality; however, the available light was limited because all the windows were situated on the same wall. To overcome this problem, medium-height furniture and translucent panels were incorporated to illuminate the apartment as much as possible. The large size of the loft allowed for spacious functional areas, which were designed in keeping with the airy ambience of the place. The elegantly furnished kitchen is situated along one of the walls, thus opening up the space. The light table sits at one end of the room, and the living area is beside the windows and the chimney. Simple translucent fiber panels divide the day areas from the bedroom and permit the flow of natural light, while interior fluorescent lights illuminate the bookcase.

Location: New York City, New York, USA › Completion date: 2003 › Photos: © Jordi Miralles

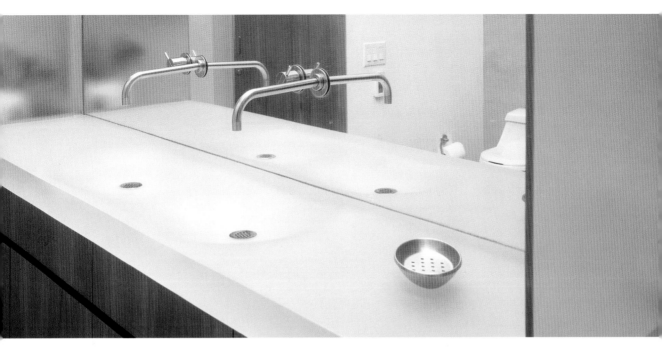

Plan

The minimalist en suite bathroom oozes intimacy. The sink, the side panels, and the lamp are all made from resin.

The study comprises a light table and a flat filing cabinet.
An innovative metallic panel, on which photos can be displayed
magnetically, contributes to the loft's unique personality.

Dwelling in Brussels

Architect: Johanne Riss

☐ In addition to being a residential space, this expansive, evocative loft also serves as a Belgian fashion designer's studio. The apartment possesses a certain delicacy, reflecting a sensibility also expressed in the owner's work. The loft exudes creativity with a careful selection of materials and colors and the subtle fusion of different styles of furniture. The loft's interior is further characterized by industrial elements, such as the roof beams and skylights, which let in ample natural light. The rooms are divided by shelving and medium-height panels, producing a feeling of greater space and accentuating the height of the dwelling. This sensation is enhanced by the predominant use of the color white throughout the loft, which creates a calm yet carefree environment. The designer's studio is situated on the lower floor, where mannequins dressed in the designer's creations and photographs of models emphasize the studio's originality. An interior pond draws inspiration from tranquil Asian gardens and provides a unique touch.

Location: Brussels, Belgium › Completion date: 2005 › Photos: © Laurent Brandajs

The interior pond fills the room with a delightful Asian aura.
The mannequins clothed in the owner's designs
intensify the originality of the space.

Studio in Madrid

Architect: A-cero

☐ The present-day loft concept embraces different types of dwellings. The original premise of an old industrial space converted into a studio-style apartment has been transformed to include newly built apartments, in which the floor plan is not completely open. In this project, however, all the characteristics of a genuine loft have been achieved. This two-story loft boasts a 14,500-square-foot upper floor reminiscent of its industrial past. The principal objectives of the project were to maximize the exposure to natural light and distribute the space to best practical and esthetic effect within the somewhat chaotic metal structure. The bedrooms and bathrooms were located at the sides, with the kitchen, dining room, and large living room in the center. At one end a glass wall takes advantage of the peace and tranquility transmitted through the interior garden-patio. The predominantly white walls and beams contrast with the black touches in some of the furniture, which was designed by the architects, and in the kitchen. Red accents throughout add color and vitality to the whole.

Location: Madrid, Spain › Completion date: 2005 › Photos: © Santiago Barrio

A glass wall allows natural light to flow through the apartment from the interior patio. Below, the entrance hall on the ground floor is decorated in white.

A large table, designed by the architects adapts to the space. Its shape can be altered to accommodate a comfortable and elegant sofa.

McCollum Loft

Architect: **Roy Leone Design Studio**

☐ This loft, located in the Soho district of New York City, was once a honey storeroom and is housed in one of the typical nineteenth-century structures that characterize the neighborhood. The structure and interior features, such as the steel columns, transmit an industrial feel, which adds personality to the loft, and serve as a backdrop for the new elements. The perimeter walls were preserved to emphasize the contrast of old and new; in addition, two windows were incorporated into the western wall to increase the apartment's natural light. To maintain an open floor plan and enable the different zones of the apartment to be reorganized, a new space was added to accommodate the kitchen, bathroom, and dressing room. The living room, dining room, bedroom, and hallway are all situated in a single space. A metal-and-acrylic panel, which sets off the small living room, and a linen curtain surrounding the bed create a feeling of greater intimacy. The linen curtain also serves as a screen onto which images can be projected to be viewed from the bedroom or living room.

Location: New York City, New York, USA › Completion date: 2003 › Photos: © Eduard Hueber/Archphoto

The linen curtain visually sets off the bedroom area from the rest of the apartment. A projector can display images on the fabric, which and gives the décor a dynamic edge.

1 ENTRY
2 LIBRARY
3 DINING
4 KITCHEN
5 LAUNDRY
6 BATH
7 DRESSING
8 SLEEPING
9 LIVING

0   5   10   20

N —

Plan

Fitted bookcases fully exploit the great heights of this loft. The
columns, as well as being a structural element, also convey a retro
esthetic, creating an interesting contrast with the modern furniture.

Loft in Milan

Architect: **Francesca Donati Studio**

☐ This original loft, situated on the outskirts of Milan in a peripheral zone where agriculture and industry coexist, is both the residence and study of the owner/architect. The building was originally a stately home, located beside a granary, a windmill, and a series of annexed warehouses, one of which was used for this project. The structure, in keeping with the industrial architecture of the turn of the century, is characterized by the smelted iron beams and the brick walls. The original structure has been respected in the creation of this flexible, light-filled, and perfectly habitable space. All the private areas are contained in a mezzanine, including the bedroom, the bathroom, and even a place for a future sauna, while the study is located on the ground floor. Natural light flows in through a large skylight and through two sizable glass doors, allowing for a warm and pleasant working area. Although the decorative scheme is austere, it maintains this feeling of comfort, particularly at night.

Location: Milan, Italy › Completion date: 2001 › Photos: © Andrea Martiradonna

The glass panels in the mezzanine counteract the weight
of the structure and allow light to flow in. The bed
and much of the furniture are made from masonry.

Loft in Ciutat Vella

Architect: Maria Vives, Lluís Escarmis/GCA Arquitectes

☐ This loft, located in the heart of the city center, preserves industrial features and elements. The arched brick ceiling and the iron columns with decorative cornices are typical of late-nineteenth- and early-twentieth-century industrial architecture. The large dimensions of the building facilitates the distribution of the rooms without worry about space. The day area consists of a large living room, a kitchen, a dining room, and a small, elevated study. The furniture, including well-known designer pieces such as the Verner Panton chairs and the Le Corbusier chaise longue and armchairs, provides an interesting contrast with the existing industrial elements. In the master bedroom, a glass wall allows natural light to flow through into the living room, creating visual continuity. A custom-made piece has been used as a headboard, which also serves as a panel to conceal the bathroom. Both bedrooms have en suite bathrooms. The industrial past and modern-day life coexist in this attractive urban space.

Location: Barcelona, Spain › Completion date: 2002 › Photos: © Jordi Miralles

In the living room, the fusion of industrial
elements and contemporary furniture results
in an attractive, cutting-edge interior.

Plan

The bricks and original arched ceiling convey warmth to the predominantly black-and-gray space. Large paintings and photographic art decorate the walls.

Loft Kortrijk

Architect: Decruy & D'hont

☐ The distribution of functional areas in this large loft maintains a contemporary feel throughout the interior, in part due to the sturdy, metal staircases that connect the different levels and give the space a "factory premises" air. The rooms themselves have high-quality finishes and elegant décor, despite the generally informal style. The floor of the entrance hall is polished cement, whereas the rest of the flooring is parquet. The spacious and well-equipped kitchen boasts a small dining area with chairs in various complementary hues. Simple, translucent panels separate the kitchen from the sizable living room and allow the flow of light between them. The red sofas and chairs and the chipboard dining table lend the space a hospitable feel. The artwork adorning the walls creates a sophisticated and cosmopolitan environment, and the red details in some of the decorative touches add strength and character to the loft.

Location: Brussels, Belgium › Completion date: 2003 › Photos: © Laurent Brandajs

The metal staircases with their straight lines are striking visual
elements and take on a near sculptural quality.

Loft in a Textile Factory

Interior designer: Sara Folch

☐ This apartment is a fine example of the loft as a transformation of industrial space into a living area. A former textile factory is now a perfectly appointed urban residence with an undeniable industrial ambience, evident in the arched ceilings, the metal beams, and the style of the columns, all features of Barcelona's old industrial architecture. The juxtaposition of this historic building with the modern furniture and floor plan create a pleasant and warm whole. The white walls and furniture work beautifully with the high ceilings and give the apartment a truly spacious air. The white color extends to the kitchen, while the wooden floors give the space a sense of comfort and warmth. The rectangular floor plan puts the living room and study at one end of the loft, with the kitchen and dining room in the center. The bedroom is situated on a slightly elevated level and succeeds in being intimate without partitions or other forms of enclosure.

Location: Barcelona, Spain › Completion date: 2002 › Photos: © Jordi Miralles

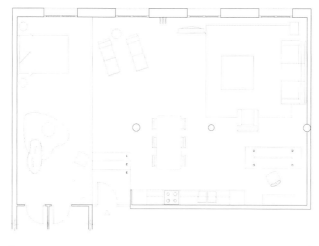

Plan

The kitchen and the large dining room table are closely linked and also set off the living room and the bedroom.

The bedroom is separated visually from the rest of the
loft as a result of the height differential. The unfussy décor and
curtains, which filter the light, create an alluring corner.

Domestic Warehouse

Architect: Popoff-Bouquelle

☐ This loft was created with a greater focus on structural expression than on actual construction. The floor plan was designed around a central interior patio, which also had a bearing on the distribution of the different rooms. The owners' needs determined the choice of materials such as cement and concrete, which, along with the columns, lend an industrial air to the apartment. The windows are built into glass walls, which maximizes the flow of light into the apartment. A series of cabinets with folding doors are distributed throughout the loft, which serve to define, reveal, or conceal the different rooms such as the kitchen, hidden behind one of the units. Similarly, the work area is set off by a bookcase, likewise exemplifying the way new spaces and atmospheres can be introduced. Bright, shiny colors combine to bring vitality and warmth to this otherwise rather cold space. The bedroom is situated between tall wardrobes that act as a dividing wall to allow for privacy without isolating the room completely.

Location: Brussels, Belgium › Completion date: 2002 › Photos: © Laurent Brandajs

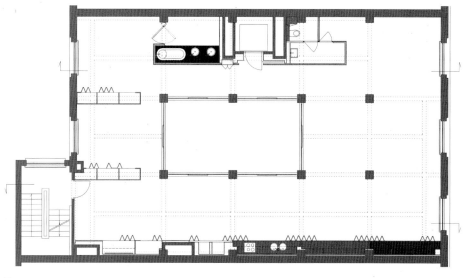

Plan

The bathroom is one of the few truly private areas of the apartment.
The dark gray color creates an intimate environment, which
contrasts with the completely open plan of the loft in general.

Ammann Loft

Architect: Delphine Ammann/N-bodyarchitektenag

☐ Located in the Swiss town of Frauenfeld, this loft has the large dimensions necessary to allow for the interior design to be tailored to the owner's individual needs. The kitchen sits within a red-colored cube-shaped area, which contrasts with the intense black theme of the overall space and, because it does not quite reach the ceiling, accentuates the height of the loft. The kitchen segues into a hall by means of the doors at either end, which lends a feeling of continuity to the whole living area. If desired, the kitchen can be completely closed off, and the elegant living room thus becomes the focal point. The bedrooms, each with an en suite bathroom, are connected to the rest of the rooms, optimizing ease of movement. The bedroom partitions, which likewise do not quite reach the ceiling, serve as dividers, with doors incorporated into the wall. A color scheme based on black, red, and white, along with the stylish furniture, work together to create a distinguished and subdued loft, with the large table and chairs lending it the feeling of a professional office.

Location: Frauenfeld, Switzerland › Completion date: 2001 › Photos: © Reto Guntli/Zapaimages

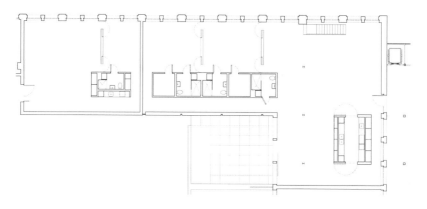

Plan

Metallic beams give the loft an edge of strength and robustness. The layout incorporates dividers that can be used to create different areas within the living space around the pillars.

Black and white complement a bedroom consisting of
pure and simple lines and further enhance the creative
use of shapes and volumes in this room.

Distribution
and Color

Loft in Vienna

Architect: **Johannes Will/Will Manufaktur Architektur Moebelkultur**

☐ This 1,900-square-foot loft is located in a nineteenth-century Viennese building. The restricted palette of colors and materials accentuates the openness of the loft, in which the purity of lines and shapes creates an extremely simple, bright, minimalist space. The massive windows running along the length of the outer wall flood the apartment with natural light, and the wooden floors and lounge furniture add warmth. The starkness of the lines is repeated in the shapes of the furniture—the long, elegant table, the plain sofas, and the living room's simple lamps. The master bedroom is separated from the living room by a large upholstered wall, and the integrated swing door becomes a decorative element, owing to its striking design. The kitchen is a well-appointed and ample space, decorated with wood and metal finishes. A glass wall permits an exterior view while working and creates a feeling of greater expansiveness in the hallway.

Location: Vienna, Austria › Completion date: 2003 › Photos: © Paul Ott

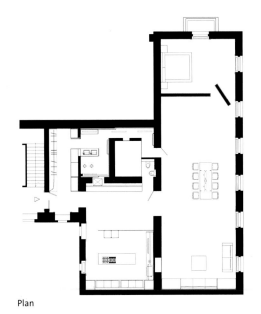

Plan

The well-designed kitchen is a high point. Its generous size and
the glass wall magnify its spaciousness.

Miami Beach Pied-à-Terre

Architect: Pablo Uribe/Studio Uribe

☐ This small loft was designed for a couple who already have a house set back from the seafront in Miami Beach. The loft was therefore envisaged as a second home, somewhere to have a shower or informal dinner after a day at the beach, or simply a place to spend the night after the evening concerts. Because of the sporadic use of the apartment, the project was simplified so that all household functions could be integrated into a single space. The existing interior walls were eliminated to gain space. The floor is polished cement and the windows are aluminum, bringing simplicity and elegance to the interior, and drawing inspiration from the building itself, which was constructed in 1967. The kitchen is situated inside the entrance hall next to the dining area and leads into the living room and a small work area. The bedroom and bathroom are located on one side. Positioning the bed opposite the sofa creates a sensation of amplitude and continuity through out the space. This loft also features a small balcony, which is almost completely taken up by a brick bench.

Location: Miami Beach, Florida, USA › Completion date: 2003 › Photos: © Claudia Uribe

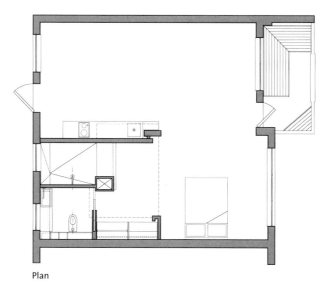

Plan

The use of light shades of color creates a summery ambience, enhanced by the colors of some of the furnishings, which add freshness and vitality.

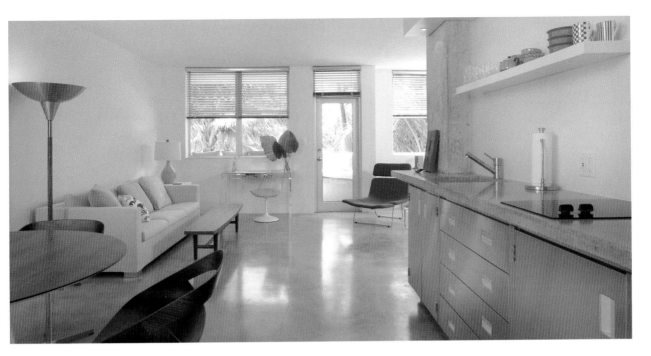

Loft Louise

Architect: Jean Leclercq/Delices Architectes

☐ This former office was rehabilitated so that it could be converted into dwelling space. The open spaces that characterized it have been maintained, as has the expansive rectangular floor, which is one of the attractions of this apartment. The only enclosed space is the dynamic bedroom area, which is surrounded by glass walls that can be either transparent or opaque, depending on the circumstances. The architects describe these walls as luminous, strange, and erotic. The lounge boasts a fireplace which adds warmth and coziness to this elegant loft. Another important element of the décor that has been carefully studied is light, sources of which range from a small corner lamp to the large windows that maximize the flow of natural light. Most of the flooring is stained wengue wood; however, the kitchen and bathroom floors are steel or ceramic tiling in anthracite shades, materials that add character to a somber interior.

Location: Brussels, Belgium › Completion date: 2002 › Photos: © Laurent Brandajs

The bathroom combines gray mosaic tiling with a white sink and bath, an elegant and timeless combination.

Gonsalves Apartment

Architect: Smart Design Studio

☐ This loft is characterized by a distinctive 1950s esthetic, as well as by the spectacular views of the harbor, which have been converted into the principal design elements of the project. The works of Alvar Aalto were studied to find an appropriate context for the work of the architects, and an intense geometric style was adopted, which is most evident in the use of the circular ceiling lights. The loft is based on the principles of simplicity, clarity, and strength. A new kitchen, bathroom, and wine cellar were included, all following the same scheme of dark-colored walls and floors. Most of the furniture, as well as other furnishings such as rugs, sofas, tables, and beds, were made especially for this project in order to maintain a revisionist décor characteristic of the 1950s. The project thus represents a fusion of architecture, interior design, and product design, resulting in a simple yet sophisticated loft where each room has been meticulously designed to avoid monotony.

Location: Elizabeth Bay, New South Wales, Australia › Completion date: 2004 › Photos: © Sharrin Rees

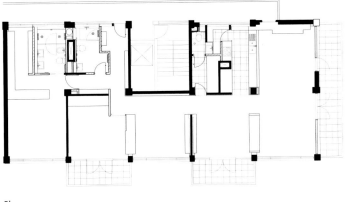

Plan

The circular ceiling lights are used throughout the loft and adhere to a modern and original esthetic.

Black as the central theme of the kitchen, as well as
other elements such as the tables and sofas, creates
a sophisticated and elegant ambience.

Loft for a Young Executive

Architect: **Brunete Fraccaroli**

☐ The architect Brunete Fraccaroli designed this 5,900-square-foot loft for a dynamic and modern executive, and succeeded in reflecting both qualities in the apartment. The interior has been given vitality by combining and contrasting materials such as glass and steel or wood and synthetics, as well as by the bold use of color. The automatic and sliding doors introduce technology to the apartment, further represented by the rotating plasma television situated within a panel separating two rooms so that it can be watched from both the living room and the bedroom. Other elements of this apartment, such as the textured glass plates and the sisal wallpaper, reflect the architect's own innovative ideas. The bathroom is worth a special mention for its unique and extravagant design, which includes mirrors that multiply an image an infinite number of times, a Japanese ofuro bath, and a glass passageway with a platform on top of a rail. The combination of wood and the color green make this one of the most audacious rooms in the loft.

Location: São Paulo, Brazil › Completion date: 2002 › Photos: © Tuca Reinés

A green glass wall and mobile panels separate the living room from the bedroom. The plasma television rotates easily and can be watched from anywhere.

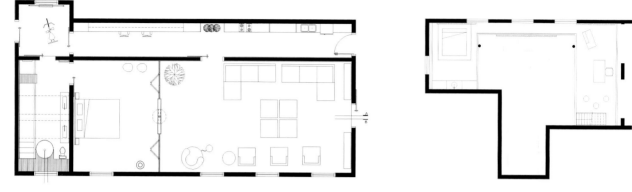

Plans

In this room, personal care takes on a special meaning. A small gymnasium situated next to the bathroom converts this area into a place for rest, relaxation, and pampering the body.

The kitchen, situated along the length of the corridor, is in tune with the esthetic of the rest of the loft in terms of its innovative materials and stark contrast of colors.

New York Unit P-18A

Architects: John Friedman Alice Kimm Architects

☐ This Manhattan apartment is located in an old building that formerly housed a department store. The roof is unusually high for this type of building, though this encourages a feeling of greater openness and space. The previous floor plan was fragmented and choppy and the high ceilings accentuated the narrowness of the rooms, so all the walls were eliminated to create a more open environment, resulting in an interesting collage of different ceiling heights. The kitchen connects to the hall area through an opening introduced into the wall, adhering to the objective of this low-budget project to create a fluid and comfortable loft. Therefore, the architect focused on scale, light, and movement, to allow colors and materials to bring a new sense of richness and texture to the interior. "Simplicity" and "elegance" are the best words to sum up the result of this transformation, where minimum furniture accentuates the fluidity between the areas and creates a visual continuity throughout the apartment.

Location: New York City, New York, USA › Completion date: 2002 › Photos: © Michael Moran

Ben Avigdor Lofts

Architect: Avi Laiser & Amir Shwarz – U-I

☐ This one-time diamond-polishing factory houses lofts designed and constructed by U-I. The building is located within a growth area that is attracting artists, designers, and other young professionals, transforming it into a fresh and dynamic district. The primary objectives of the project were architectural innovations on a low budget to be carried out within a short period of time. Five diversely sized units were built in such a way to enable them to be increased or decreased in size with ease, at a later date. The floors are polished cement and each area's color varies in accordance with its use. The bathroom surfaces are made from plywood, a material highly resistant to water and humidity, and constitute another innovative feature of these lofts. As soon as the lofts were completed, they were snapped up by a writer, an architect, and a graphic designer, among others.

Location: Tel Aviv, Israel › Completion date: 2005 › Photos: © Miri Davidovitch

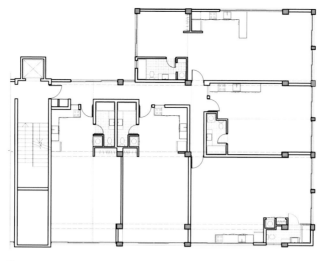

Plan

The polished cement flooring lends a modern and urban aspect to the loft. The feeling of spaciousness is created by eliminating superfluous elements.

The simple furnishings adapt to the lifestyle of the tenants,
who are primarily young and independent professionals.

Loft Building in Los Angeles

Architect: Kerry Joyce Associates

☐ The restoration project of the Gas Company buildings is an ambitious project that also involves the rehabilitation of the surrounding area. The building, constructed in 1924 by the architects Parkinson & Parkinson, was the precursor for a decisive era of development in the city of Los Angeles. In 1942, its extension by architect Robert Derrah combined a minimalist style with art deco. In the conversion of these former offices into three distinctly styled lofts, Kerry Joyce was in charge of the interior design and blended a variety of styles and features to create extremely elegant and cutting-edge interiors. One solution was to use modern coatings and finishes such as polished concrete and whitened wood for the enormous original windows and doors. Floor plans were carefully designed. One of the spaces is delineated by large white circles joined together by clips, giving a modern and airy feel. Another apartment radiates warmth and coziness, owing to the wooden furniture.

Location: Los Angeles, California, USA › Completion date: 2004 › Photos: © Dominique Vorillon

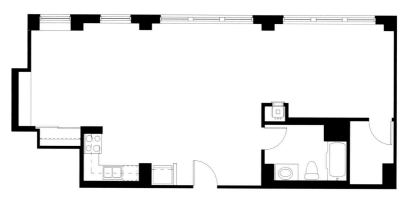

Plan

The color white is a central theme in the décor of this loft.
The rugs and cushions give the impeccable
and luminous space a cozier quality.

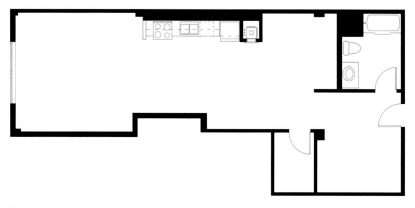

Plan

The distribution of space in the second loft allows for the incorporation of a small work area. The use of wood in the décor lends warmth to the interior.

Loft Willens

Architect: Alain Borgers, Philippe Dumoulin/Edena Architects

☐ This spacious and luminous loft is characterized by the flow of one functional area into the next—for example, the sizable living room is situated in the same space as the kitchen and dining area. The design of the furniture and its careful placement define each area and give the apartment its character. A large glass wall that looks out onto a small terrace maximizes the flow of natural light. At one end of the space a modern chaise longue sits alongside shelves filled with books, creating an inviting reading corner. The simplicity of the kitchen and its accoutrements enable it to be integrated into the space without distorting the overall esthetic. The absence of tall furniture creates spatial continuity, and the high ceilings accentuate the depth of the loft. The palette of colors is another main player in the interior decoration; the contrasting light and gray colors permeate the apartment, from the bathroom to the living room.

Location: Brussels, Belgium › Completion date: 2002 › Photos: © Laurent Brandajs

The dining room table is situated between the kitchen and the
large glass wall, benefiting from its closeness to
the kitchen and the presence of natural light.

Fasan Dwelling

Architect: **Johannes Will/Will Manufaktur Architektur Moebelkultur**

☐ Reducing the dwelling to its essential functions can produce an apartment with features created by the space itself and the imaginative use of light and shadows. This 5,900-square-foot loft is characterized by emptiness, the fluidity of space, and the concentration of the basic elements of the apartment. To obtain these clear lines, the walls and openings were eliminated and subtle, light-connecting areas were created. One of the most outstanding elements is the fragmentation of the main wall that creates a connecting area without walls between the bathroom, kitchen, and living room. The opening is a sculptural, three-dimensional shape, which gives the loft character and a robust edge. To achieve the esthetic harmony that pervades this loft, all kitchen appliances are concealed behind handle-free sliding panels. The precision of the design is the result of attentive planning and quality materials such as glass, metal, and wooden panels. These elements combine to produce a highly individualized interior.

Location: Vienna, Austria › Completion date: 2004 › Photos: © Paul Ott

The clean lines in the bedroom do not detract from the feeling
of warmth. The consistency of the light and the warmth of the
wooden wall create a minimalist, yet hospitable, environment.

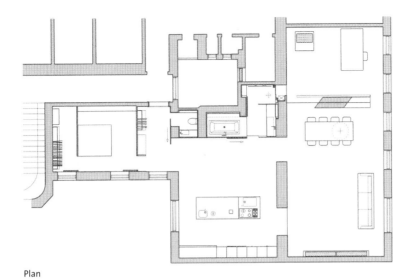

Plan

The glass wall that separates the bathroom from the kitchen adds depth to the space. This element defies the conventional design of bathrooms, where privacy is the goal.

The combination of colors, the texture of
the wood, and the purity of the lines result in
bathrooms that are both somber and elegant.

Patrolia Loft

Architect: William Ruhl/Ruhl Walker Architects

☐ Although not directly apparent, this modern apartment has been adapted for wheelchair users, which means that the interior had to be modified according to a rational plan. However, the urban and sophisticated lifestyle of the owner was also a major influencing factor in the interior design. Certain modifications have been carried out to optimize mobility within each space in a clear and direct manner, without concealing the solutions. Another of the objectives was to balance the esthetic with the practical needs, and this loft is a perfect example of how any given requirement can be met without neglecting design. This concept is exemplified by the kitchen work surface which is on two levels to enhance ease of use. A wall diagonally cuts across the floor area and accentuates the depth of the loft. The day area and the private rooms are connected by a ramp, as they are located on different levels. The bathroom is also adapted to the owner's personal needs, with a freestanding sink and a shower area that is situated on a slight slope.

Location: Boston, Massachusetts, USA › Completion date: 2004 › Photos: © Edua Wilde

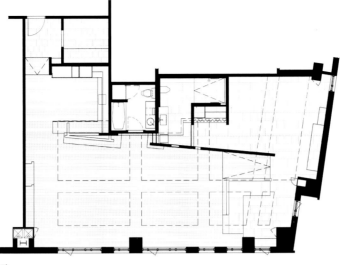

Plan

The study, situated on a level above the living room and kitchen, offers a view that surveys practically the whole loft. Work and home are fused into a practical and esthetically pleasing solution.

T House

Architect: Riegler Riewe Architekten

☐ This top-floor apartment, a new construction located above an urban residential and commercial building, is the starting point for a project of space reorganization. The bedrooms face east and have a pleasant, calming view, whereas the large living room, utility, and infrastructure areas are all west facing. A large glass wall parallel to the utility area opens the space up fully onto the town and defines limits between interior and exterior, city and dwelling. Maximizing the entry of light is always a principal objective in the design of dwellings in Central European countries, and in this case the clarity created by the large windows results in a dynamic day space full of vitality. Mobile panels permit the flow of light into certain areas of the loft and also enhance the flexibility of the spaces by creating additional rooms, depending on their position and the individual needs of the owners. A lightweight staircase on the balcony leads up to an extensive terrace with a larchswood floor.

Location: Graz, Austria › Completion date: 2004 › Photos: © Paul Ott

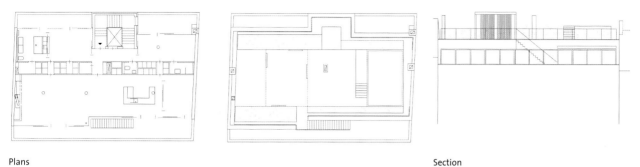

Plans

Section

The red color of the central area's walls and the parquet flooring add warmth to the interior of this luminous loft.

The exterior of the apartment is covered in sheets of larchwood, a very light material with resistant qualities. In the background, a stairway leads to a small pool.

Loft in Tel Aviv

Architect: Alex Meitlis Architecture and Design

☐ This architect's loft is on the top floor of an industrial building situated on a busy Tel Aviv street, where old industrial buildings coexist alongside workshops, shops, restaurants, and cafés. The apartment is clearly divided into two distinct zones: the architect's study and the living area. The zones are connected by a meeting room, which is separated from the living room by a large glass wall. The element of simplicity and the color white accentuate the lightness of the interior. The floor is shiny white resin, the iron windows are painted white, and the custom furniture, designed by the architect, is also white. This central theme of white was chosen because of its ability to soothe and relax the overworked eyes of an architect whose daily task involves constant consideration of shapes, materials, and colors. The height of the ceilings, accentuated by the columns and the size of the furniture, helps create a feeling of spatial continuity. Careful selection of furnishings and decorative objects add to the personality of this loft.

Location: Tel Aviv, Israel › Completion date: 2003 › Photos: © Yael Pincus

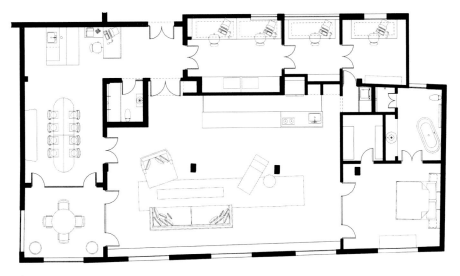

Plan

The color white also plays a part in the bedroom
and the master bathroom, creating environments
that evoke lightness and modernity.

Panels and Partitions

Wasch Residence

Architect: Alden Maddry

☐ This building was formerly a hotel and more recently a photographic studio, before being acquired by the present owners. The distribution of the entire space was redesigned, and walls and separations were eliminated to transform it into an apartment. The dining room and kitchen lead into the living room, where a quick breakfast or informal meal can be enjoyed at a small bar. Translucent sliding panels with resin detailing give the loft a dynamic quality, revealing a second living room, which amplifies the apartment and can also be used as an intimate guest bedroom. The principal aim was to maximize the amount of light, hence the use of transom windows, which improve the air circulation and take full advantage of the high ceilings. The modern furniture and color schemes produce an inviting atmosphere.

Location: New York City, New York, USA › Completion date: 2005 › Photos: © Seong Kwon

The master bedroom is viewed from the living room, which can be transformed into a guest bedroom. The mobile resin panels are shown on the right in the photo.

The floor plan of the loft unites the living room and dining room day areas. A small study positioned alongside the dining room makes for a peaceful workplace.

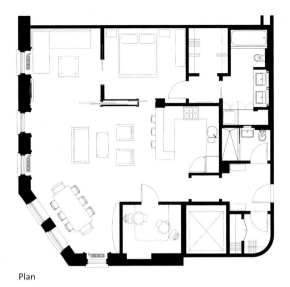

Plan

The colorful décor and the mobile
windows and panels give the interior of
this comfortable, elegant loft a dynamic edge.

McGrath Apartment

Architect: Anima

☐ This apartment in the Chelsea neighborhood has been transformed into an elegant and functional loft. The elongated floor plan was modified to eliminate all the walls, thus converting it into a flexible uninterrupted space, suffused with light. The most public areas of the loft—the hall, kitchen, and office/guest bedroom—are situated at the entrance, whereas the master bedroom and the bathroom are located at the opposite end. Sliding doors emphasize the straight lines and vertical nature of the space. Custom closets are concealed behind translucent glass doors. The professional-looking kitchen has an industrial feel to it as a result of the stainless steel décor and its custom furniture, inspired by the folding Swiss Army knife, that reveals or conceals the appliances as desired. The small bathroom is decorated with blue mosaic tiles and glass, transforming it into an efficient and elegant space.

Location: New York City, New York, USA › Completion date: 2003 › Photos: © Paul Rivera/Archphoto

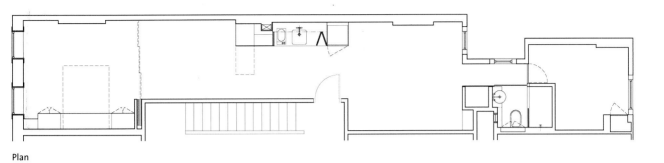

Plan

The kitchen is situated at the center of the apartment,
which, thanks to its custom quality design, blends
perfectly with the esthetic of the loft.

Despite being the smallest room, the blue shades and smoked glass door give the bathroom a distinguished air.

Loft in Melbourne

Architect: Six Degrees Architects

☐ This nearly square-shaped loft was reorganized to house the essential functional areas such as the bedroom, bathrooms, kitchen, and living room. The versatile space allowed for multiple possibilities but also required a carefully planned design to achieve freedom of movement, an outstanding feature of the loft. A single, gray structure serves as a wall, separating the bedroom from the kitchen area and preserving privacy in areas such as the bathroom, without the existence of a door. The floor plan incorporates a kitchen that opens out onto the living room and dining area. Distinctive types of flooring visually separate each space—polished cement in the living room and bedroom, a parquet platform in the kitchen, and mosaic tiles in the bathroom. The décor is somber but by no means cold, and the combination of shades of gray with the luminosity of the white walls enhances the character of this loft.

Location: Melbourne, Australia › Completion date: 2004 › Photos: © Shania Shegedyn

The combination of materials and textures creates a serene ambience in the bathroom. The shades of blues and grays and sthe original use of pebbles evoke a tranquil environment.

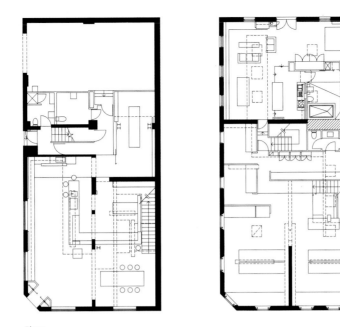

Plans

L Loft

Architect: William Ruhl/Ruhl Walker Architects

☐ The existing space in this loft was transformed to create an open plan suffused with natural light. The rectangular loft was subdivided into different functional areas by using varied materials, changes in level, and mobile translucent partitions. The glass wall, which cuts across the loft diagonally to separate the living area from the master bedroom, is a notable feature. The master bedroom sits on a wooden platform, creating a cozy ambience of warmth and comfort, whereas the rest of the floors are polished cement. The private space behind the glass wall is made up of a bedroom and bathroom. There is a small desk between the day and night zones, which participates in both areas. In the spacious lounge, a curved wall with fitted shelving stands out, accentuating the depth of the space. The elegantly appointed wood-paneled kitchen integrates smoothly with the living area and adds a warm touch to the loft's décor.

Location: Boston, Massachusetts, USA › Completion date: 2004 › Photos: © Edua Wilde

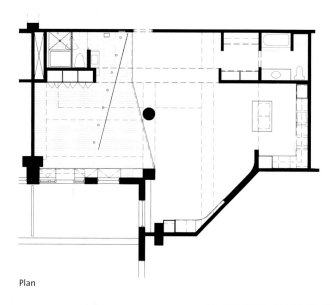

Plan

The kitchen is fitted with light-colored wooden cabinets. The back wall is made of stainless steel. The table in front of the stove can be used as a work counter or as an informal dining area.

Egg Loft

Architect: Angelica Ruano, Pierre Nicolas Ledoux/Plain Space

☐ The construction of this loft called for remodeling one of the floors of a former office and commercial building. The existing floor plan consisted of a series of small spaces with low ceilings, which impeded the light flow. Therefore, to expand the space, all the pipes were relocated on the perimeter and the ceilings were made higher. The new plan integrates all the spaces and allows them to be closed off when greater privacy is desired, by use of discreet mobile panels. Materials and colors were selected to optimize the flow of natural light to the whole apartment. Previously, the adjacent building was visible from the window in the master bedroom, so it was necessary to minimize this view and reduce the noise level. This was resolved by using a translucent glass pane that lets in the light and acts as a sound barrier. Although the interior decoration is rather somber, the innovative oval shape, which conceals a small television room, and the colored lighting help create a more individualized space.

Location: New York City, New York, USA › Completion date: 2004 › Photos: © Paul Rivera/Archphoto

The kitchen can be concealed by simply lowering the panels, whose translucent material allows the light to flow, indirectly illuminating the living area.

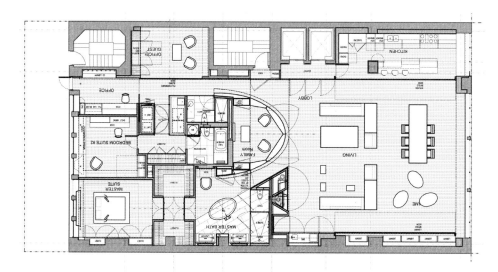

Plan

A sheet of glass serves as both headboard and panel, thus minimizing the exterior view. The plants form a natural curtain and give the room a more hospitable feel.

Loft in Caldes de Montbui

Interior Design: Manel Torres/In Disseny

☐ Although this diaphanous yet small space of approximately 750 square feet has no real partitions, the project design allows for it to be divided into two areas: the entrance hall, through which the kitchen is located, and the living room, which is visually differentiated from the dining room by a bookcase. The only dividers are the small false walls, such as the one that separates the dining room from the kitchen, and the sliding door of the bedroom. The bedroom is situated next to the living room and although the en suite bathroom has no door, it is well concealed within the space. The modern furniture and its careful placement result in an attractive and dynamic loft with plenty of character, thanks to the creative use of color. All sides of this apartment face the exterior, and it is surrounded by a balcony, which magnifies the feeling of space by flooding the apartment with light.

Location: Caldes de Montbui, Spain › Completion date: 2005 › Photos: © Stephan Zahring

The kitchen counter contains a small but clever sliding table, which increases the overall area of the work surface.

A large sofa and glass coffee table create a simple yet comfortable living area from which the entire loft can be appreciated. The roller blinds filter the light flowing through the windows.

The materials used in the bathroom create an elegant and serene space where the false wall, which separates the bath from the bedroom, also serves as a headboard.

Gershon Loft

Architect: Jeff Etelemaki/Jeff Etelemaki Design Studio

☐ This inviting one-bedroom loft is the result of the remodeling of commercial premises in the Flatiron District of New York. Large-scale changes were made, and the surface areas were altered with the aim of connecting the two ends of this elongated loft. The central utility area has been fitted with wooden panels of silver fir, which conceal a storage area consisting of cupboards and an office. A large, U-shaped bookcase, also in silver fir, creates a peaceful reading corner at one end of the hallway, farthest from the kitchen and living areas. Custom-made steel structured sliding panels, which isolate and separate the bedroom from the day area, maintain the sensation of open space and allow light to penetrate through to the kitchen. The furniture and décor succeed in integrating all the spaces into a single warm and homey atmosphere. A lighting system similar to those found in art galleries highlights the works of art and photographs that decorate the loft's walls.

Location: New York City, New York, USA › Completion date: 2004 › Photos: © Steve Williams

Plan

The hallway contains cupboards and wooden
panels, optimizing the use of space and also
creating a greater feeling of warmth.

Van Beestraat Residence

Architect: Marc Prosman Architecten

☐ This spacious loft is housed in a building that has served as a stable for horses, a tram shed, and later as a college for midwives. The loft has been transformed into a residential space without losing sight of its origins, and some of its more characteristic elements have been preserved. The owner wanted the day area to be integrated into a single space and the bedrooms to have a certain level of intimacy. Some of the furniture was custom-made, such as the desk, the kitchen furniture, and the sturdy bronze table in the ample space behind the original glass door. The living area is situated upstairs, which gives the space an interesting perspective and separates it from the rest of the functional areas. The master bedroom and study are accessed by way of the kitchen, and the pasageway can be closed off by means of wooden panels. The bathrooms have simple and pure lines and are decorated in white marble. This project proves that traditional materials such as stone, glass, and wood can acquire new connotations and significance through precise design.

Location: Amsterdam, Netherlands › Completion date: 2004 › Photos: © Christian Richters

A good perspective of the kitchen and the windows overlooking the garden can be obtained from the living room. Thanks to the windows that run all the way around the loft, a great quantity of natural light floods into the space.

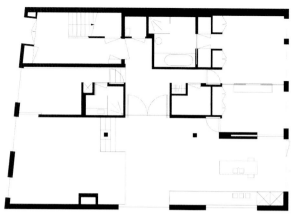

Plan

An elegant wooden panel separates the kitchen and the study and also isolates the master bedroom. The warmth of the material serves to integrate this partition into the space.

NY Loft

Architect: Stefania Rinaldi/Studio Rinaldi

☐ This loft was designed to accentuate luminosity and open space, which are fundamental characteristics of this kind of apartment. The height of the ceiling was an advantage in this approach. The rooms are divided by panels and partitions to maintain continuity between spaces. The translucent glass doors allow for both flexibility and privacy in the dwelling and contribute to the dynamic environment. The custom furniture, made from materials such as walnut wood and aluminum, defines the elegant and simple style of this loft. The master bedroom includes a large en suite bathroom into which light flows through sliding windows. This room is also decorated with walnut wood furniture and features light shades and a floor tiled in marble with mosaic and terrazzo. The kitchen opens out onto the living room and dining area, creating a place for informal family gatherings. The consistency of the décor adds to the graceful proportion of this loft.

Location: New York City, New York, USA › Completion date: 2004 › Photos: © Wade Zimmerman

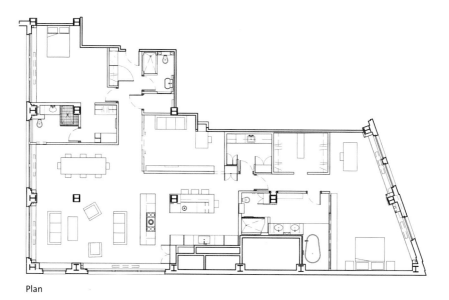

Plan

The bathroom is an elegant space with an interesting contrast of colors. The walnut wood furnishings set off the various matte tiles.

N House

Architect: Studio Damilano

☐ This elegant two-bedroom apartment is divided into individual areas by means of panels and partitions that create unique and versatile spaces. A glass wall separates the dining area from the living room, resulting in a framed effect that is apparent from both sides. The use of the color white and the nearly pure lines add serenity and luminosity to the ambience. Another panel of wooden sheets divides the dining area from the loft's entrance, and a third partition similarly separates the kitchen from the rest of the apartment. Transparency and light are fundamental to the interior design of this loft, evident in the white walls and sofas that bring the kitchen to life. Dark-colored wood has been used for contrast, adding a note of distinction. In the bathroom, the glass walls of the shower also set off the bathing area, which sits on an elevated level. The absence of superfluous elements allows serenity and tranquility to emanate from this loft.

Location: Cuneo, Italy › Completion date: 2003 › Photos: © Michele De Vita

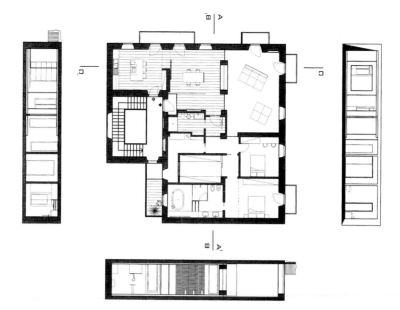

Plan

Flatiron Loft

Architect: James Slade/Slade Architecture

☐ The renovation of this apartment was dependent on the needs of the owner, a fashion designer interested in the history of design as well as industrial design. The loft houses the owner's personal possessions, so unusual materials were chosen to express his own esthetic, to catch the attention of visitors and awaken their sensibility. A further aim was to fill the interior with natural light, which was achieved by using translucent panels that slide on small wheels, thus opening up or concealing the different zones as needed. The kitchen boasts a freestanding mobile piece that serves as a bar and can be moved to the lounge in order to free up kitchen space. Some of the kitchen furniture was made using a material originating from recycled paper and some from translucent acrylic materials. Wooden panels that slide along rails serve to conceal elements of the lounge. The hallway is accented with translucent surfaces that create interesting reflections of light. The loft also features a bedroom that stands out for its simplicity and a bathroom with a magnificent onyx sink.

Location: New York City, New York, USA › Completion date: 2003 › Photos: © Jordi Miralles

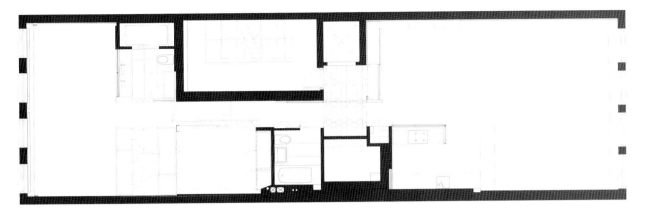

Plan

The glass panels create an Asian-inspired airy ambience. The light quality adds a touch of elegance to the hallway.

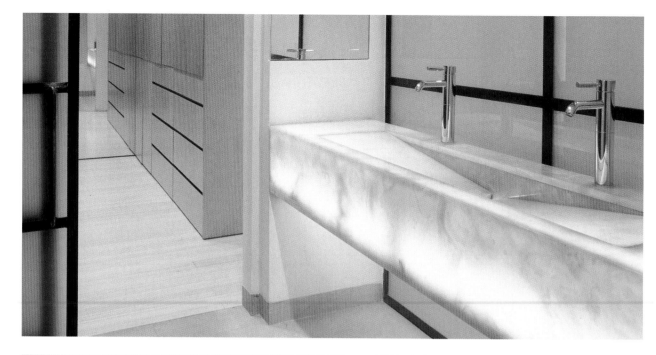

Panels with leather ties set off a small study. To heighten the intimacy of the guest bathroom, translucent panels were used.

Directory

A-cero Estudio de Arquitectura y Urbanismo SL
Arriaza 6 bajos
28008 Madrid, Spain
T. +34 915 489 656
F. +34 915 489 657
a-cero@a-cero.com
www.a-cero.com
Studio in Madrid

Alden Maddry
928 Lorimer Street, Suite 3
Brooklyn, NY 11222, USA
T. +1 718 383 1947
F. +1 718 360 0487
 am@aldenmaddry.com
www.aldenmaddry.com
Wasch Residence

Alex Meitlis Architecture and Design
2 Vital Street
66088 Tel Aviv, Israel
T. +972 3 6814734
F. +972 3 6823499
studio@alexmeitlis.com
Loft in Tel Aviv

Anima
20 Jay Street, Suite 308
Brooklyn, NY 11201, USA
T. +1 718 643 1123
F. +1 718 643 0905
justin@anima.cc
www.anima.cc
McGrath Apartment

Avi Laiser & Amir Shwarz – U-I
6 Meytav Street
67898 Tel Aviv, Israel
T. +972 3 5625440
F. +972 3 5621639
avilaiser@hotmail.com
Ben Avigdor Lofts

Brunete Fraccaroli Arquitetura e Interiores
Rua Guarará 261 7º andar Jd. Paulista
01425-001 São Paulo, Brazil
T. +55 11 3885 8309
brunete@osite.com.br
www.brunetefraccaroli.com.br
Loft in São Paulo
Loft for a Young Executive

Daniele Geltrudi
Via Cadinal Tosi 10
21052 Busto Arsizio, Italy
T. +39 349 1263102
dgeltru@tin.it
RP Apartment

Decruy & D'hont
16 Guido Gezellelaan
8800 Roeselare, Belgium
T. +32 51 69 00 23
F. +32 51 69 00 24
patrickdhont.buro@telenet.be
yvesdecruy.buro@telenet.be
www.decruy-dhont.be
Loft Kortrijk

Delices Architectes
81 Avenue Paul Deschanel
1030 Brussels, Belgium
T. +32 2 216 36 19
F. +32 2 216 06 77
info@delicesarchitectes.com
www.delicesarchitectes.com
Loft Louise

Edena Architects
23 Rue des Glands
1190 Brussels, Belgium
T. +32 2 346 20 08
F. +32 2 343 14 80
edena@skynet.be
Loft Willens

Francesca Donati Studio
Via Corelli 34
20134 Milan, Italy
T. +39 02 70 20 01 93
francescadonatistudio@yahoo.com
www.francescadonati.it
Loft in Milan

GCA Arquitectes
València 289 baixos
08009 Barcelona, Spain
T. +34 934 761 800
F. +34 934 761 806
info@gcaarq.com
www.gcaarq.com
Loft in Ciutat Vella

Guita Maleki & Pascal Cheikh Djavadi
110 Boulevard de Clichy
75018 Paris, France
T./F. +33 1 4252 5364
guita.ma@wanadoo.fr
Apartment in Marais

In Disseny
Pi i Margall 81
08140 Caldes de Montbui, Spain
T. +34 938 655 446
www.indisseny.com
Jorge Rangel
www.jorgerangel.com
Loft in Caldes de Montbui

Joan Pons Forment
Llull 47-49 àtic 4.ª
08005 Barcelona, Spain
T. +34 933 170 128
M. +34 670 856 261
Loft in Born

Joan Bach
Passeig de Gràcia 52 pral.
08007 Barcelona, Spain
T. +34 934 881 925
F. +34 934 871 640
joan.bach@coac.net
Fraternitat Duplex
Frankie Loft

Johanne Riss
35 Place du Noveau Marché aux Grains
1000 Brussels, Belgium
T. +32 2 513 09 00
F. +32 2 514 32 84
johanneriss@johanneriss.com
www.johanneriss.com
Dwelling in Brussels

John Friedman Alice Kimm Architects
701 East Third Street, Suite 300
Los Angeles, CA 90013, USA
T. +1 213 253 4740
F. +1 213 253 4760
info@jfak.net
www.jfak.net
New York Unit P-18A
Gershon Loft

Jeff Etelemaki Design Studio
10 Jay Street, Suite 308
Brooklyn, NY 11201, USA
T. +1 718 243 9088
F. +1 718 243 0454
info@je-designstudio.com
www.je-designstudio.com

Kerry Joyce Associates
115 North La Brea Avenue
Los Angeles, CA 90036, USA
T. +1 323 938 4442
F. +1 323 938 0484
info@kerryjoyce.com
www.kerryjoyce.com
Lofts Building in Los Angeles

Manuel Serrano Arquitectos
Padilla 54 nave
28006 Madrid, Spain
T. +34 913 093 635
F. +34 913 093 633
arquitectura@serrano-arquitectos.net
www.serrano-arquitectos.net
Loft in Madrid

Marc Prosman Architecten
Overtoom 197
1054 HT Amsterdam, Netherlands
T. +31 20 489 2099
F. +31 20 489 3658
architecten@prosman.nl
www.prosman.nl
Van Beestraat Residence

N-bodyarchitektenag
Ausstellungstrasse 41
8005 Zürich, Switzerland
T. +41 43 205 2630
F. +41 43 205 2631
M. +41 797 537 424
delphineammann@yahoo.com
www.n-body.ch
Ammann Loft

Plain Space
139 Fulton Street, Suite 719
New York, NY 10038, USA
T. +1 347 892 2617
F. +1 347 952 4729
aruano@plainspace.net
Egg Loft

Popoff-Bouquelle
57 Rue des Commerçants
1000 Brussels, Belgium
T. +32 2 648 41 17
entrepot_domestique@skynet.be
Domestic Warehouse

Raphaël Orts, Nicolas Balleriaux
183 Rue Franz Merjay
1050 Brussels, Belgium
T. +32 2 344 58 63
F. +32 2 344 58 63
raphael.orts@tiscali.be
m.balleriaux@scarlet.be
Van Gelder Loft

Riegler Riewe Architekten
Griesgasse 10
8020 Graz, Austria
T. +43 316 72 32 53 0
F. +43 316 72 32 53 4
office@rieglerriewe.co.at
www.rieglerriewe.co.at
T House

Roy Leone Design Studio
10 Jay Street, Suite 308
Brooklyn, NY 11201, USA
T +1 718 243 9088
F +1 718 243 0454
rleone@royleone.com
www.royleone.com
McCollum Loft

Ruhl Walker Architects
60 K Street
Boston, MA 02127, USA
T. +1 617 268 5479
F. +1 617 268 5482
info@ruhlwalker.com
www.ruhlwalker.com
Patrolia Loft
L Loft

Sara Folch Estudi d'Interiorisme
Plaça Sant Vicenç de Sarrià 12 2.º 1.ª
08017 Barcelona, Spain
T. +34 932 800 428
F. +34 932 800 428
sarafolch@yahoo.es
Loft in a Textile Factory

Six Degrees Architects
100 Adderley Street, West Melbourne
PO Box 14003
8001 Melbourne, Australia
T. +61 3 9321 6565
F. +61 3 9328 4088
www.sixdegrees.com.au
Loft in Melbourne

Slade Architecture
367 East 10th Street
New York, NY 10009, USA
T. +1 212 677 6380
F. +1 212 677 6330
www.sladearch.com
Noho Loft
Flatiron Loft

Smart Design Studio
632 Bourke Street
2010 Surry Hills, NSW, Australia
T. +61 2 8332 4333
F. +61 2 8332 4344
info@smartdesignstudio.com
www.smartdesignstudio.com
Residence in Surry Hills
Gonsalves Apartment

Studio Associato Bettinelli
Via Carrozzai 6b
24122 Bergamo, Italy
T. +39 35 235796
F. +39 35 225941
bettinellistudio@bitbit.it
Loft in Bergamo

Studio Damilano
Via Pratolungo 1
12100 San Rocco Castagnaretta, Italy
T./F. +39 0171 49 35 04
damilano@libero.it
N House

Studio Rinaldi
250 West 57th Street, Suite 1210
New York, NY 10107, USA
T. +1 212 581 2314
F. +1 212 581 2524
www.studiosrinaldi.com
NY Loft

Studio Uribe
1225 Lenox Avenue
Miami Beach, FL 33139, USA
T. +1 305 695 1415
design@studiouribe.com
www.studiouribe.com
Miami Beach Pied-à-Terre

**Will Manufaktur Architektur Moebelkultur
Johannes Will GmbH**
Großglobnitz 47
3910 Zwettl, Austria
T. +43 2823 228
F. +43 2823 228 19
www.willl.at
Loft in Vienna
Fasan Dwelling